Just Marriage

Just Marriage

for Better, for Worse, FOREVER

Bonnie Louise Kuchler

WILLOW CREEK PRESS

Published by Willow Creek Press
P.O. Box 147, Minocqua, Wisconsin 54548

For information on other Willow Creek Press titles,
call 1-800-850-9453

Photo Credits
p5 © WILDLIFE GmbH/Alamy; p6 © Ron Kimball/www.kimballstock.com; p9 © Jagdeep Rajput/ardea.com;
p10 © Alaska Stock LLC/Alamy; p13 © Ron Kimball/www.kimballstock.com; p14 © ARCO/C. Huetter/age fotostock;
p17 © tbkmedia.de/Alamy; p18 © JUPITERIMAGES/Comstock Premium/Alamy; p21 © M. Watson/ardea.com;
p22-23 © Ryan McVay/Photodisc/Alamy; p25 © C. Huetter/Arco Images GmbH/Alamy; p26 © Juniors Bildarchiv/Alamy;
p29 © Juniors Bildarchiv/age fotostock; p30 © WILDLIFE GmbH/Alamy; p33 © Juniors Bildarchiv/age fotostock;
p34 © Richard Stacks/www.kimballstock.com; p37 © Juniors Bildarchiv/Alamy;
p38 © Per-Andrea Hoffman/LOOK Die Bildagentur der Fotografen GmbH/Alamy; p41 © RF Company/Alamy;
p42 © Ron Kimball/www.kimballstock.com; p44-45 © Steve Bloom Images/Alamy; p46 © Top-Pics TBK/Alamy;
p49 © Biosphoto/Gilson François/Peter Arnold Inc.; p50 © Robert Franz/www.kimballstock.com;
p53 © Biosphoto/Puillandre Roger/Peter Arnold Inc.; p54 © Denver Bryan/www.kimballstock.com;
p57 © Klein Hubert/www.kimballstock.com; p58 © David Osborn/Alamy.com; p61 © WILDLIFE GmbH/Alamy;
p62 © Linda Freshwaters Arndt/Alamy; p65 © Ron Kimball/www.kimballstock.com; p66 © blickwinkel/Alamy;
p69 © Biosphoto/Thiriet Claudius/Peter Arnold Inc.; p70 © Ron Kimball/www.kimballstock.com; p73 © Kevin Schafer 2009;
p74 © John Lund/www.kimballstock.com; p77 © Richard Stacks/www.kimballstock.com p78-79 © Juniors Bildarchiv/age fotostock;
p81 © Marten Dalfors/Alamy; p82 © John Pitcher/Design Pics Inc./Alamy; p85 © Juniors Bildarchiv/Alamy;
p86 © Steve Bloom Images/Alamy; p89 © Biosphoto/Koenig Christian/Peter Arnold Inc.;
p90 © Biosphoto/Klein J.-L. & Hubert M.-L./Peter Arnold Inc.; p93 © Alaska Stock LLC/Alamy;
p95 © C. Huetter/Arco Images GmbH/Alamy

Printed in Canada

"I do."

No two words in the English language
are spoken with more excitement,
more anticipation,
or more strings attached.

"I now pronounce you man and wife."
With the possible exceptions of "We have lift-off" and
"This country is at war," there are few phrases as sobering.
—*Erma Bombeck*

With two tiny words, you have
vowed to share all of your heart.

Happiness is not so much in having as sharing.
We make a living by what we get,
but we make a life by what we give.
—*Norman MacEwan*

You've pledged to share
all of your home.

Marriage is an alliance entered into by a man
who can't sleep with the window shut, and a
woman who can't sleep with the window open.
—*George Bernard Shaw*

And you've sworn to share all of
your decision-making power.

In my house I'm the boss,
my wife is just the decision maker.
—*Woody Allen*

For one magical moment,
with one simple oath,
bride and groom have joined
together and two halves
become a whole.

Marriage is like twirling a baton, turning
hand springs, or eating with chopsticks.
It looks easy until you try it.
—*Helen Rowland*

This oath allows you to mature.

Women hope men will change after
marriage but they don't; men hope
women won't change but they do.
—*Bettina Arndt*

It takes about a week for couples to realize
they must grind off each others' edges, if the
two halves are ever going to fit together.

I figure that the degree of difficulty in combining two lives
ranks somewhere between rerouting a hurricane
and finding a parking place in downtown Manhattan.
—*Claire Cloninger*

If two become one,
the question is, which one?

Kissing is a means of getting two people so close together
that they can't see anything wrong with each other.
— *Rene Yasenek*

Separate wills tug and pull,
neither wanting to yield ground.

Neither of us entered marriage thinking it wouldn't be a strain. Life has strains in it, and he's the person I want to strain with.

—*Patricia Arquette*

A good marriage grows
from a pair of forgivers.

No man ever got the better of his wife
in an argument without regretting it.
—*William Kaye*

Marriage combines two species.
One who can see muddy
footprints in a dark room,
and one who can't see mud at all,
unless it fills a wrestling pit.

It was a mixed marriage.
I'm human, he was a Klingon.
—*Carol Leifer*

A wife can always tell where
in the house her husband has been.

There are exceptions, but over 85 percent of all
males are legally classifiable as Cleaning Impaired…
If your live-together relationship is going to work,
both of you must be sensitive to the
special needs of the Cleaning Impaired.

— *Dave Barry*

Women splash homes with sweet smells,
lively colors and fluffy pillows.
Men splash bathrooms.

All marriages are happy.
It's the living together afterward
that causes all the trouble.
—*Raymond Hull*

In fact, a key ingredient of marital success is separate bathrooms.

Mold (mold) noun, verb
1) What a wife will desperately attempt to do to her husband's manners, hygienic practices, and housekeeping habits.
2) What will grow on a husband's shower curtain when the wife fails in this attempt and they finally get separate bathrooms.

—*Tom Carey*

Separate kitchens wouldn't hurt either.

Sometimes I wonder if men and women really
suit each other. Perhaps they should live
next door and just visit now and then.
—*Katharine Hepburn*

The secret to a happy marriage—
even more important than separate
bathrooms—is kindness.

Just be considerate, accept each other for what you
are, and don't point out that the hair he's losing
on his head is now growing out of his nose.
—*Peg Bundy*

Marriage is a unique competition
where the opponents hold hands.

We always hold hands. If I let go, she shops.
—*Henny (Henry) Youngman*

Couples often disagree on how to spend
money. One wants to pay bills;
the other wants to go to Hawaii.

An extravagance is anything you buy
that is of no use to your spouse.
—*Unknown*

Some couples disagree on food.
For instance, one sees a pig
and thinks of bacon or pork chops.
The other sees a pig and wants to take
her home and name her Porkchop.

I came from a family that considered gravy a beverage.
He ate vegetables, which I regarded as decorations for
the mantel. Imagine spending the rest of your life with
a man who had never had cold dumplings for breakfast!
—*Erma Bombeck*

Many couples disagree in the bedroom.
The ideal time for this, of course, is when
each is too tired to form a coherent sentence.

❤

Marriage is the only war in which
you sleep with the enemy.
—*François, Duc de La Rochefoucauld*

The first years of marriage are the toughest.
It's a time for adjustments.

Getting married for sex is like buying
a 747 for the free peanuts.
—*Jeff Foxworthy*

The newlywed phase is an enlightening time, when the blinders fall off. Spouses see clearly, for the first time, who or what they vowed to cherish.

Love prepares you for marriage the way needlepoint prepares you for round-the-world solo yachting.
—*Kathy Lette*

When a wife gets comfortable with her husband, she lets her hair down.

Keep your eyes wide open before marriage,
and half-shut afterwards.
— *Benjamin Franklin*

When a husband gets comfortable,
he burps, farts, and spits.

If your husband starts acting up, you can't
take him back to his mama's house.
*"I don't know; he just stopped working.
He's just laying around making a funny noise."*
—Wanda Sykes-Hall

A man may be a fool and not know it,
but not if he is married.
—*H.L. Mencken*

That's when spouses realize that the critical
task of changing their partners is up to them.

Given the success rate of this task,
compared to the persistence of
those attempting it, one might
conclude that marriage eats brain cells.

I love being married…
It's so great to find that one special person
you want to annoy for the rest of your life.
—*Rita Rudner*

Marriage is a powerful institution.
Those committed to it can be
transformed into two-year-olds.

Basically my wife was immature.
I'd be at home in the bath,
and she'd come in and sink my boats.
— *Woody Allen*

Transformed couples are easy to spot.

With a good marriage argument, if you do it right,
you should reach the point where neither of you have
the vaguest recollection what the original disagreement was,
but both of you are willing to get divorced over it.
—*Dave Barry*

Mature spouses, however, respond to conflict with more dignified behavior.

The problem with people who have no vices
is that generally you can be pretty sure they're
going to have some pretty annoying virtues.

—*Elizabeth Taylor*

Matrimony comes with a built-in
test that reveals which of you is
more pigheaded than the other.

We've always compromised in our marriage.
Sometimes we do things your way;
other times we don't do them mine.

—*Gene Perret*

Marriage holds the best and
the worst life has to offer.
Sometimes both
on the same day.

More marriages might survive if
the partners realized that sometimes
the better comes after the worse.
—*Doug Larson*

Married life reveals how opposite
the opposite sex really is.

When women are depressed,
they either eat or go shopping.
Men invade another country.
It's a whole different way of thinking.
—*Elayne Boosler*

This mysterious attraction of opposites
has a scientific explanation.
It's called "temporary brain dysfunction."

Men are from Earth.
Women are from Earth.
Deal with it.
—*George Carlin*

Spouses have entirely different needs.
Women need to talk, cuddle, talk, share
feelings, talk, be cherished, and talk.

You just never know when and where
to bite, blow, kiss, pat, or rub.
Women should come with directions.

—*Bill Cosby*

Men need really big televisions.

Women speak because they wish to speak;
whereas a man speaks only when driven to speech
by something outside himself—like, for instance
if he can't find any clean socks.

—*Jean Kerr*

It's true that many husbands are
listening-impaired. Coincidentally,
an equal number of wives are
silence-impaired.

The difference between a successful marriage
and a mediocre one consists of leaving
about three or four things a day unsaid.
— *Harlan Miller*

Sigmund Freud once said, "What do women want?"
The only thing I have learned in fifty-two years is that
women want men to stop asking dumb questions like that.
—*Bill Cosby*

When a husband cannot read
his wife's thoughts, she huffs.

When a wife cannot read her husband's
thoughts, he is pleased.

When a man brings his wife flowers
for no reason, there's a reason.
—*Molly McGee*

For all its failings, marriage is an
unrivaled bond. When you fall out
of love, it can hold you together
until you fall back in again.

A successful marriage requires falling in love
many times, and always with the same person.
—*Mignon McLaughlin*

There's no denying that marriage is hard work. But at the end of the day, there's also comfort. You know that someone has your back—protecting, scratching, soaping, or rubbing.

The married are those who have taken the terrible risk of intimacy and, having taken it, know life without intimacy to be impossible.
—*Carolyn Heilbrun*

Being married means you can count
on a hug when you really need it.

To keep the fire burning brightly, there's one easy rule: keep the
two logs together, near enough to keep each other warm and far
enough apart—about a finger's breadth—for breathing room.
Good fire, good marriage, same rule.

—*Marnie Reed Crowell*

Now and then you catch a glimmer of the person you fell in love with, and you remember why you said "I do" in the first place. That's when marriage is pure bliss.

I could've missed the pain,
but I'd have had to miss the dance.
—*Garth Brooks*

Through the years together, you love,
you laugh, you cry, you bang your head
against the wall, and you love again.

Wasn't marriage… like life itself, a mixture of the
sordid and the magnificent; of mud and stars;
of earth and flowers; of love and hate and laughter
and tears and ugliness and beauty and hurt.
— *Edna Ferber*

Then finally, while rummaging through
a lifetime of memories, you realize that
two heartbeats have joined into one.

There's this place in me where your fingerprints still rest,
your kisses still linger, and your whispers softly echo. It's the
place where a part of you will forever be a part of me.
—*Gretchen Kemp*

And you say
"I still do."

Grow old along with me! The best is yet to be.
—*Robert Browning*

The
End